"Chase your dream and make your life an adventure."

-Ruben Gonzalez

Ruben Gonzalez
Salt Lake City Olympics 84 MPH

FIGHT FOR YOUR DREAM

How to Develop the Focus, Discipline,
Confidence and Courage
You Need to Achieve Your Goals

by
Four-time Olympian
Ruben Gonzalez

Olympia Press

Fight for Your Dream

By Ruben Gonzalez

ISBN-10: 0975554735
ISBN-13: 978-0-9755547-3-9

Olympia Press
832-689-8282

What other Top Achievers are Saying about Ruben Gonzalez' Work

"Ruben Gonzalez achieved what few people ever do: mastery of his will. Motivating and inspiring."

Dr. Stephen Covey - Author "The 7 Habits of Highly Effective People"

"Ruben speaks from both his head and his heart, and inspires ordinary people, convincing them they can do extraordinary things. He is persuasive, enthusiastic and very real. Invite him to present his ideas to your group and you will glad you did."

Zig Ziglar - Author "See You at the Top"

"No Olympian I have ever met has more of what makes a champion than Ruben Gonzalez. Read and internalize, and you will realize and materialize your own dreams!"

Dr. Denis Waitley - Author "The Psychology of Winning"

"If you will read this book or listen to Ruben speak, your life will change for the positive."

Lou Holtz -
Legendary Notre Dame Football Coach Author "Winning Every Day"

"This is truly a blueprint to success. Read it, apply its timeless lessons, and you'll transform your dreams into reality."

Bob McEwen - U.S. Congressman

"Ruben teaches us that once we transform our fear into energy we begin to transform our dreams into reality."

Gerhard Gschwandtner - Founder and Publisher, Selling Power Magazine

"Ruben knows the steps to success. His enthusiasm and positive attitude are contagious!"

Mark Victor Hansen -
Co-creator "Chicken Soup for the Soul"

"Ruben's not only earned his spurs, but he's for real. His thankful spirit and his humble attitude, makes him one of the most wonderful speakers, most genuine speakers I have heard in my life and I recommend him with all my heart to you."

Charlie "Tremendous" Jones –
Author "Life is Tremendous"

"Ruben Gonzalez' exciting story of hard work, dedication and commitment – leading to success and achievement in the greatest competition in the world – is inspiring and uplifting in a wonderful way!"

Brian Tracy - Author "Million Dollar Habits"

"Ruben is a testament to the power of the human spirit. His book is a passionate call to action, challenging you to be the best that you can be. Through his amazing Olympic story, Ruben will inspire you to pursue your dream, equip you to get through the struggle and encourage you on to victory."

Rudy Ruettiger – Inspiration for the blockbuster movie "Rudy"

"Inspirational! Ruben has a unique ability to motivate and challenge his audiences. His compelling story about triumph over adversity on the road to the Olympics provokes us all to set and reach lofty goals."

Jack Canfield –
Author "The Success Principles"

"Practical advice that will energize and empower you to succeed. Ruben hits you with the absolute truth about what it takes to succeed in the real world."

Jim Rohn -
America's Foremost Business Philosopher

"Ruben's message of Determination, Commitment and Persistence struck home with our sales organization. His Inspirational message proves he is a winner not only in the greatest sporting competition of all, but also in team motivation. He is living testament to the concept of "Never Quit"!

Jerry Farmer -
VP North American Sales Xerox

"Terrific! Ruben is a true Rhino! His crystal-clear vision of success cuts through all boundaries. Ruben challenges us to do more, be more, take more chances, and ultimately live life to the max."

Scott Alexander -
Author "Rhinoceros Success"

"Ruben Gonzalez' life confirms an age old truth; determination, faith and believing in your God given abilities are still some of the keys to personal success."

Wally Amos -
Author "The Cookie Never Crumbles"

"If setting high goals is part of what your organization must do to succeed, you cannot do better than to hear Ruben's story. Perseverance, focus, mentorship…he drives home the importance of each of these elements in a manner that is so approachable, listeners cannot help but be motivated to reach higher and strive for more, from themselves and those around them."

Colonel Thomas Gibson - Commander 10th Air Base Wing US Air Force Academy

Congratulations.

You've just taken a step towards making your dreams a reality. Most people wish about their dreams and talk about their dreams but don't act on their dreams. Just the fact that you are investing in yourself shows you are *doing* something to get you closer to your dream.

Zig Ziglar said that you have to be before you can do and you have to do before you can have. By investing in yourself you are becoming more capable of reaching your dream. You're stacking the odds in your favor.

This Book Could Change Your Life

(But only if you apply it's information)

Here are five tips to help you turn this information into habits that will change your life:

Read this book more than once. I've read both "Think and Grow Rich" and "The Magic of Thinking Big" every year for the last 20 years. The more times you read a book, the more you become like the book.

Underline and make notes. Have a pen and highlighter in your hand. Underlining specific lines and paragraphs will triple your retention rate. Write your own thoughts in the margins and own this book.

Re-read your underlines. Re-read your key items over and over. Record and listen to your notes.

Apply the material immediately. Doing so will help you understand the material better. Don't try to be perfect. Done is better than perfect.

Prioritize what you want to learn. Select 1-3 things from the book, apply them faithfully and make them a habit.

The #1 question people ask me after listening to my presentations is:

"How can I be more successful and get better results in everything I do?"

This book is the answer to that question.

Contents

You Were Designed For Greatness

Great people were not born great. They became great by making a decision to pursue their dream in life and by refusing to give up. The struggle we must all face on the road to our dreams is what makes us great. Ordinary people can become extraordinary if they consistently and persistently follow the principles of success.

You could say I'm the poster child for "Ordinary to Extraordinary." I was not a gifted athlete. I became an Olympian through perseverance. I just refused to give up.

Step one to success is realizing that even though we might be programmed for mediocrity, we were designed and created for extraordinary achievement.

Reprogramming our minds for extraordinary achievement is simple but not easy. The road to huge successes in all areas of your life can be broken down to five steps:

1) What you say to yourself
2) Your beliefs and thoughts
3) What you do
4) Your habits
5) Your results

What you tell yourself influences what your beliefs and thoughts are. Your thoughts determine what you do. What you do repeatedly becomes your habits. Your habits determine your results. If you are not happy with your results, change what you say to yourself and surround yourself with people who support and encourage the quest for your dream. If you do that, before long you'll be getting different results.

You can learn to unlock your special powers to attract whatever you want in your life. It's just a skill.

Successful people constantly talk about and think about what they want. Unsuccessful people constantly talk about and think about what they don't want. How about you?

What do you constantly think about?

What do you always talk about?

Is it what you want or what you don't want?

Who are you spending most of your time with?

Are they focusing on the dreams or on the nightmares?

Did you know your income is the average income of the people you spend most of your time with? Want to double your income? Start hanging around people who make twice what you're making.

Seriously.

How to Fuel Your Desire to Win

There are many facets to success. You have to have a dream – something you're shooting for. You have to believe in yourself. You have to take massive action with an attitude that you are willing to do whatever it takes for as long as it takes. Then and only then is success realistic.

More than anything else, your desire will determine if you will make it. How bad do you want it? Is your dream something that you'd like to do? Is it something that would be nice to do? Or is it something that you are obsessed about?

How badly you want it will determine whether you'll realize your dream because how bad you want it determines what will make you quit.

Burning desire allows a person with average ability to successfully compete with those who have far more ability. Desire allows you to give it everything you've got. It helps you reach your full potential. Intense desire allows people to win against overwhelming odds.

If your dream is not an obsession, as soon as you come across obstacles, you'll quit. As soon as the challenge of reaching your dream becomes an inconvenience, you'll give up.

Success is not convenient. Trust me. In order to succeed you will need to inconvenience yourself in a big way - for a long time.

That's why it's so important to be driven, excited, and passionate about your dream. If your "why?" is big enough, the "how" will take care of itself.

Desire creates the power to succeed.

When I first took up the sport of luge we trained in the summer on wheeled sleds. We would slide down the Lake Placid bobsled track from the half mile point. A half mile run on a concrete track at speeds of about 50 MPH.

We wore tennis shoes, shorts, and a t-shirt. If we crashed, it was straight to the hospital. That's the weeding-out process in the sport of luge. When we got to the bottom, they did not even give us a ride back to the top. We had to carry our sleds back up the mountain. The coaches made it hard on purpose. They wanted to know right away how bad we wanted it. They didn't want to waste any time with anyone who was not serious.

If you've ever played football, you know exactly what I mean. The first couple of weeks of football practice each season are brutal. The coach works the players to death because he wants to find out who his real team will be. He wants to cull out all the wanna-bees.

To succeed, you need to know how to feed your desire. The more you feed your desire, the harder it is to quit. Most of the mental training we do is designed to do two things – to strengthen our belief level, and to fuel our desire.

You have to get yourself to the point to where no matter what your circumstances are, you are 100% focused on the dream. You want to become so determined to reach your goal that you convince yourself that you will have it. When the dream is big enough, the facts don't count.

How do you do that? How do you turn your dream into a magnificent obsession?

You surround yourself with the dream. You put pictures of your dream all around you. The walls in my office are completely covered with Olympic memorabilia. One day I counted how many sets of Olympic rings were staring at me all day long. There were over 30 sets of them. By surrounding myself with the dream, all day long I'm bombarding my mind with where I want to go. If I daydream, I daydream Olympics.

I read about the Olympics all the time. I watch Olympic videos all the time (I have over 200 hours of Olympic videos). Most importantly, I allow myself to get emotional about my dream. Many times when I'm watching the videos – especially Opening Ceremonies videos – my eyes well up with tears.

If you want something badly enough, the facts don't count.

I talk to everyone about my dream. I regularly speak with other athletes that are in the hunt. I think about my dream all day long and I dream about my dream all night long.

I vividly imagine what it's going to feel like when I'm walking into the Opening Ceremonies. I can hear the people cheering. I can see the Olympic flag and Olympic torch. I can feel the cold air and the snow hitting my face. I can feel the tears of joy. I can feel the goose bumps. Vividly imagining what it's going to feel like feeds my desire.

Writing about my dream is a powerful exercise. Whenever you put your thoughts down on paper your mind gets very focused and intense.

Pro and Olympic athletes aren't the only ones to use these techniques. If you're married, you've probably done many of these things. When you first fell in love, you constantly thought about your love, you had pictures of him or her around you all the time. You wanted to know everything about them. You wrote letters to her. You constantly talked about her to your friends. In fact, they were probably sick of hearing you talk about him or her. You were obsessed!

And what happened? You probably ended up getting married.

A child that wants a puppy does the same thing. They talk about puppies. They read about puppies. They think about puppies. They collect pictures of puppies. And eventually, the parents break down and buy the puppy.

Do the same with your dream. Get obsessed! Become a fanatic! Obsessed fanatics make dreams come true. If I could do it, you can do it.

Is there something you want so badly you'd die if you didn't have it?

If there was something you could want so badly, what would it be?

Do you have a dream that takes your breath away?

What kind of dream would take your breath away?

Once you discover your dream, dedicate your life to its pursuit.

How to Use Your Strengths to Win More

Have you ever been in a situation where work seemed effortless? Well, you were probably in a situation that required you to use your personal strengths.

Socrates said "Know thyself." Socrates was right on the money. Knowing your strengths and weaknesses makes your success journey faster and easier. The better you understand what your strengths are, the better equipped you are to come up with a strategy that will help you win in life.

Success is pretty simple. In order to achieve success you need to find an arena you are suited to play in. After that, you have to have the guts to get started, the guts to endure through the challenges you'll inevitably face, and along the way have an attitude that you're willing to do whatever it takes for as long as it takes to get the job done.

The first part of success is finding an arena you're suited to play in. In order to do that, you have to know your strengths and weaknesses. The better you know yourself, the more you'll know your potential for peak performance in any arena.

This concept applies in sports, in education, at home, in your personal and in your professional success.

In sports, knowing yourself is not as complicated. Your body type rules out many sports. Someone built like a linebacker will not make an effective wide receiver. I would not make a good sumo wrestler or a good jockey. Your speed, agility, jumping power, strength, and your specific skills further narrow what sport you might excel in.

Successful people focus on their strengths. Do you know yours?

If you've ever played football, your coaches tested you to determine what position you were best suited for. It saved time and it was plain smart.

In school, many counselors give aptitude tests to help students figure out what profession they might enjoy and be best suited for.

If you're in sales for a major corporation, you've undoubtedly taken personality tests when you interviewed for a job. The sales manager wanted to know if your personality matched the set of qualities found in the most successful salespeople.

If you're in management, you've probably taken similar tests so your boss would know whether you might have what it takes to manage others – and if you did, what management style you would have.

If I had not known what my strengths were, I never would have made it to the Olympics. As I tell my audiences, I was not a great athlete. My main strength was perseverance. I chose the sport of luge because I knew I could persevere in the face of challenges. I figured the luge was dangerous enough that there would be many quitters.

My strategy was to outlast the competition. I never would have been able to come up with a strategy if I had not known what my strengths were.

As an Olympic athlete, I'm always looking for anything that might give me an edge over the competition.

I've found that if something helps me become a better athlete it usually also helps me in my personal and professional life. Over the years I've taken many personality tests and assessments. I understand that the better I know myself, the more I can excel.

By learning what makes me tick, I've learned what my hot buttons are – so it is easier for me to motivate myself. I've also learned what turns me off and why.

Finally, I've come to understand my communication style. Knowing your communication style is of huge importance because 85% of success comes down to your people skills. For me this knowledge about myself is invaluable because it helps keep me out of trouble and it helps me be my best.

A few years ago I took a DISC personality assessment.

The report was uncanny. It revealed things about me that I did not consciously know but that once I read them, I immediately agreed with. The report gave me insights about me that have helped me build my business and have helped me whenever I communicate with others – my wife, my children, my colleagues, my prospects, etc.

I've always worked hard. The knowledge from this report allows me to work smart as well. Bottom line, it has made me more productive. It gives me an edge. It helps me win more in life and at work.

Investing the time and money to get to know yourself will pay huge dividends. Don't wait for your boss to test you. Take the initiative to do it on your own. You'll be glad you did.

Once you know what your dream is and what your strengths are, you can start "majoring on the majors" in life. You can really start taking advantage of the 80-20 rule.

Do you know what your strengths are?

Do you realize that when people complement you that have just gotten a glimpse of your greatness? They have seen one of your strengths – something that you have probably been discounting simply because it's so natural to you. Start paying attention to people's complements. Their compliments will give you a good idea of where your strengths may be.

Then use those strengths in the pursuit of your dream.

How to Find Your Dream and Purpose

I'm going to share a sad fact with you. When I speak at an Elementary School and ask my audience, "Do you have dreams?" almost every hand goes up. When I ask the same question at a Middle School, only half of the hands go up. When I ask High School and College students if they have dreams, only a few hands go up. And when I speak to adults at conventions, or corporate events, I'm surprised if anybody raises their hand. In fact, I don't even ask the adults anymore because it just embarrasses them.

Benjamin Franklin said, "Most men die at age 25 but are not buried until they are 70." What he meant was, most people give up on their dreams before they are 30 years old, and spend the rest of their lives in "survival mode," living day to day, just trying to get through the day rather than living a life filled with passion, in the pursuit of their dreams.

Life is tough. There's no doubt about it. And unless you are crystal-clear about where you want to go, crystal-clear about your life purpose, mission, calling, or destiny, and unless you believe it is possible for you to make your dream a reality, you will not act on it and you will revert to "survival mode". Believe me, "survival mode" is not a good place to be.

I know. I've been there. Ever since the third grade, I dreamed of being an Olympic athlete. But I didn't believe in myself so I never committed to acting on my dream. Eventually I put my Olympic dream up on the shelf. For years, I felt lost. I felt like a nobody. I felt I was not making a difference. I did not like myself. Many years later, while in College, something happened that inspired me to go for it.

The whole secret to a successful life is to find out what it is your destiny to do, and then do it.

When I saw tiny Scott Hamilton win the Gold Medal at the 1984 Sarajevo Olympics, I said to myself, "If that little guy can do it, I can do it too! I *will* be in the next Olympics!" And I made a commitment to do whatever it took to make my dream a reality. All of a sudden, my life had purpose, meaning, and passion. Four years later I was marching in the Opening Ceremonies of the 1988 Calgary Winter Olympics.

I believe God puts a dream in your heart, he gives you all the gifts, talents, and resources we need to make our dreams a reality. But it's up to you to believe in yourself and it is up to you to do the work. Many times, you will not discover your true gifts until you put yourself through the struggle of chasing your dream. The person you become through the struggle is your gift back to God.

You were created to make your dream come true. It is your life purpose. It is you calling. It's your mission. Your dream will draw on your talents, it will appeal to your highest ideals, and will give you unlimited energy. Having a vision of where you want to be satisfies several universal drives within you. Having a dream connects with the spirit that dwells in your heart; it gives you an outlet for your unique gifts and talents, and makes you feel that your life matters. It makes you feel that you are making a difference.

A dream does several things. It gives you a future focus. Instead of being worried about the frustrations of the present, a dream gets you thinking about the possibilities of the future. A dream gives you energy. Have you ever been so engrossed in a book or in a project that hours seemed like minutes? That's what it feels like when you are passionately chasing your dream. Finally, a dream keeps you from wasting your life. Dreams keep you from wasting your talents, your abilities, and your creativity. They keep you from living a life filled with regret. That terrible "What might have been?" feeling.

You will experience success in life to the extent that you are clear about and commit to achieving your life purpose.

How do you find your purpose? It all comes down to spending some quality time getting to know yourself through some very specific questions. I would suggest going out by yourself for a couple of days to a quiet place, maybe a cabin in the woods, out by a lake, a place where you will not be interrupted and really thinking about it. It might be a good idea to take a notebook to write your thoughts.

Before you read the questions, think about some people you deeply admire. What is it about them that you admire? Specifically what qualities do you admire in them? I'd be willing to bet that anyone you admire, is someone who is dedicating their life to their unique calling. If you are having trouble thinking of people, just think about people like Richard Branson, Michael Jordan, Tiger Woods, Mother Theresa, Bill Gates, Sam Walton, Norman Schwarzkopf, and the NASA Astronauts.

What do they have in common? They love what they do. They would do it for free. They are good at what they do. Doing what they do is extremely important to them. They have a sense of destiny, a sense that they are doing what they were born to do.

Well you know what? The experiences you have had up to this point in your life have prepared you for your life purpose. You have unique talents, abilities, interests, and values that only you can bring to greatness. There is a destiny that only you can fulfill. But first you need to find out what you would love to do. What you would be willing to do for free. What you are good at doing. What is extremely important to you. What you were born to do.

So here are the questions. Don't just glance at them. Invest some time in them. Remember, what you learn from them could change your life – and the world. You might want to write each of these questions on a separate index card and spend at least fifteen minutes on each one. Fifteen minutes writing your unique answer in your life mission notebook.

Note - Some of these questions are very similar. They are just worded differently. This is done intentionally. I want to stimulate different parts of your brain in order to get closer to your true answer.

What are my greatest talents?

What do others say I am good at? (Weigh this heavily because many times our gifts come so naturally to us, that we underestimate them. Your true gifts will be more apparent to others.)

What have my unique life experiences prepared me to do?

What do I love to do so much that I would do it for free? Why? (The why is very important. It will give you clues to your driving force.)

What activities give me satisfaction? Why?

What excites me about life? Why?

What is my secret ambition? Why?

What are my hobbies?

What is my greatest character strength?

What is my greatest passion?

What would I be willing to die for? Why?

What will I feel like when I make it happen?

What will the regret feel like if I don't make it happen?

What am I good at?

What do I get complimented on?

Where have I excelled in the past?

Where have I been successful?

What is important to me?

What do you naturally do well?

What things do you view as your greatest successes? Why?

Is there a cause about which you feel passionate?

What is it about that cause that attracts you to it?

What are the most important lessons you have learned through your experiences about life?

What do you daydream about doing? Why?

What things do you want to be remembered for at the end of your life? Why?

What things will your life be incomplete without? Why?

If you had a year left to live, what would you do differently? Why?

What would you do if you knew you could not fail? Why?

What would you do with your time if you were wealthy? Why?

What do you stand for?

What were you born to do?

What is your unique mission in life?

What are your unique opportunities?

Where can you make a difference?

How do you want to be remembered? Why?

What will outlast you?

What will continue after you are gone?

What legacy do you want to leave behind? Why?

You might want to go through this exercise on an ongoing basis (maybe a couple of questions every day) until you become crystal-clear about your purpose in life.

Remember, you can't make your dream come true if you don't even know what it is. If you can't see it, you can't get it. Once you see it, dedicate your life to making it a reality. Give yourself to your vision. You are worthy of it. It's why you're here. It's how you will make a difference in the world. It's how you'll be remembered. It's your legacy.

So? Are you going to do this or not? Don't you dare turn the page.

If you do, you are making a big mistake.

DO THIS EXERCISE. If you don't, you have no one but yourself to blame for not realizing your dreams.

I don't care who you are. I don't care if you are a CEO or the President of the United States. I don't care if last week you climbed Mt. Everest. You need to do this. You need to find out what your next dream will be.

Otherwise you are sentencing yourself to a life of mediocrity.

Decide You Will
Get the Last Laugh

The four world-class sprinters had a dream to compete in the summer Olympics in track and field. When they failed to qualify, rather than having a pity party, they put their heads together to think of another way to make their Olympic Dream a reality. After brainstorming for solutions they decided to become bobsledders and go for the Winter Olympics.

It would be the first time a bobsled team from Jamaica would compete in the Olympics. Jamaican bobsled? "Inconceivable!" said most people. But they were great athletes - extremely fast. They just needed to master their new sport's techniques. The fact they came from Jamaica was completely immaterial. The only fact that mattered was whether they were willing to put themselves through the struggle.

I chatted with them briefly at the 1988, 1992 and 2002 Olympics. At the 88' Calgary Olympics, when they were just getting started, everyone laughed at them – sometimes to their face. They were experiencing what pioneers in every field experience – lots of ridicule. When I asked them how everyone's mockery made them feel, they replied, "Just watch us. We're not quitters. We will get the last laugh."

A few days later, during the 88' Olympic competition, they had a horrific crash (you can watch it in their Disney movie "Cool Runnings"). When you watch the crash, as the bobsled flips and smashes into the wall, it looks like the driver's neck is snapping. Incredibly, Stokes, the driver, walked away from the crash. Stokes walked away from the crash but not away from bobsledding. The Jamaicans refused to quit. They *were* going to have the last laugh.

Four years later at the Albertville Olympics, a few people were still laughing, but no longer to their face. The Jamaicans were gaining experience. By the 2002 Salt Lake City Olympics, their fifth Olympics, the Jamaicans were beating some solid teams. No one was laughing now – except the Jamaicans!

By now they had earned the admiration of people from all over the world.

What I learned from the Jamaican Bobsledders is that no matter who you are, whenever you try something new, something different, something daring and bold, people always react in the same way. At first they laugh at you, then, they watch you to see if you quit or not, and finally, if you persist and start getting results, they admire you. But it's up to you to endure while everyone else is laughing.

That's why it's so important to build a Dream Team of supporters. A group of people who believe in you and encourage you through the tough times.

Next time you are doing something bold and courageous and people are laughing at you, do what the Jamaicans did. Decide you will get the last laugh.

Are there people out there who are laughing at you? If there aren't, you're probably not doing much.

Are you willing to persist while others are laughing? Do you realize that anyone who laughs at you simply does not believe as much as you do?

Will you decide to get the last laugh? It's your choice.

30

How to Set Goals
Like a Champion

What would your life be like if failure was not an option? Would you like to perform at your peak more often? What would you do if you knew you could not fail?

Four years after making a decision to begin training for the Olympics, I made my dream come true. I competed in the 1988 Calgary Winter Olympics in the luge. I went on to compete in the 1992 Albertville Olympics, the 2002 Salt Lake City Olympics and I competed in the 2010 Vancouver Olympics at the age of 47. In Vancouver everyone thought I was a coach!

How does someone who did not even take up the sport of luge until he was 22 become a Four-Time Olympian? As I tell thousands of people in my speeches, I'm not a big shot. I'm just a little shot that keeps on shooting. I'm proof that ordinary people can aspire to achieve extraordinary things if they will just follow a few simple steps.

Step 1: Choose a goal.
Step 2: See yourself succeeding at your goal.
Step 3: Choose a quality that will help you reach your goal.
Step 4: Create a new habit that will help you achieve your goal.

Step 1: Choose a goal.

What changes would you like to make in your life that excite you just by thinking about them? What would you love to do? Where do you want to be ten years from now? What is your dream?

Ever since I was in the third grade I wanted to be an Olympic Athlete. I respected the Olympians because they were an example of what I believed in - they are willing to commit to a goal, willing to risk adversity in the pursuit of it, willing to fail and at the same time keep trying until they succeeded.

But it was not until I was in college and saw Scott Hamilton compete in the Sarajevo games that I actually made the decision to train for the Olympics.

But just thinking about your goal is not enough. If you want to reach your goal, you need to make it real by writing it down. Don't worry how you will make your dream come true at first. Magic happens when you put your goals down on paper. Writing it down is the first step in turning a dream you might achieve into a goal you will achieve.

In 1960, Harvard Business School did a study of their graduates 20 years after they had graduated. They found the top 3% moneymakers made as much money as the other 97% put together. The only difference between the two groups was the top 3% had always written and regularly read their goals. As a result, everything they did on a day-to-day basis was focused on reaching their goals.

People that Set and Regularly Review their Goals Accomplish 50-100 Times More than People Who Don't.

When Tiger Woods was a young boy, he wrote down on a 3x5 card that he intended to break all of Jack Nicklaus' records. Tiger read his card every night. Jack Nicklaus agrees that Tiger in on track to make it happen.

The most effective way to write your goals down is to take a 3x5 card and on one side write:

"I intend to (state your goal) by (date)."

On the other side of your card write why.

"I intend to accomplish this because (state your reasons)"

Write at least three reasons why you will do it. The more reasons the more you increase your belief.

Read your card first thing in the morning every day to stay focused on the objective. Then read your card every night before turning out the lights so your subconscious can work all night on ways to make it happen.

Success Tip - Read your card in front of a mirror while looking right at your eyes. Read it with passion, with energy. Whenever you say the word "I", touch your chest with your index finger. Make it like a pep talk. I guarantee that by doing it that way, you will develop tremendous desire, passion, and mental strength.

Step 2: See yourself succeeding at your goal.

Several times a day close your eyes and for a couple of minutes vividly imagine what it's going to feel like when you achieve your goal. Really get into it. Feel it as if it were really happening right now. Get excited. Your subconscious does not know the difference between imagining it and it really happening. By doing this, you become passionate about your desire, your belief becomes unshakeable and you become unstoppable.

I constantly imagined what it was going to be like when I walked into the Olympic Stadium at the Opening Ceremonies. I imagined it in great detail. I could see the crowds waving at me. I could see the flags and the balloons. I could hear the roar of the crowd, the fireworks, the Olympic Hymn. I could feel the cold wind blowing snow onto my cheeks. I could feel the tears of joy streaming down my face. I could feel the goose bumps running up my back and over my shoulders. I thought about it all the time, while jogging, while lifting weights, even in the shower. It was my dream - but it became my goal. And when I finally entered the Olympic arena, it was just the same - only 100 times better.

Seeing yourself succeeding is an important step because imagining yourself succeeding will keep you from quitting when the going gets tough.

Seeing yourself succeeding is fun. You can feel the excitement of reaching your objective – before you get there. You will feel victorious. You will feel great. But don't wait until you get there to practice feeling successful – imagine being successful now.

Step 3: Choose a quality that will help you reach your goal.

Have you ever looked at someone and wished you could be like them? Everyone has at one time or another. The good news is that if you notice a quality in someone else, you have some of that quality in yourself. You just need to develop it further. "It takes one to know one." Any quality you admire in someone else is a quality you have – you just need to practice it.

So step number three in reaching your goal is to choose the main quality you think you will need to reach your goal. Is it Boldness? Creativity? Enthusiasm? Patience? Leadership?

In my case it was Perseverance. To get good at the luge, I knew I was going to have to endure many crashes and injuries and simply refuse to give up. So I made a decision to become perseverant. To never quit. The main difference between a success and a failure is that the successful person tried one more time. I decided to persevere in trying one more time.

Step 4: Create a new habit that will help you achieve your goal.

Good habits usually don't just happen. You need to develop a specific plan for creating a new habit. It's simply a matter of choosing an action that helps develop your quality, deciding when to practice that action, knowing that you are going to have to repeat it many times and then giving yourself a reminder.

Since perseverance was the most important quality I needed to have to reach my goal, I needed to find ways to develop my perseverance. I had to get good at "not quitting." So I decided to become an expert on perseverance. I read books about people who had faced great challenges and refused to give up. The books inspired me to believe that if they could, I could too.

I made a decision that no matter how bad a crash I had, I would get back on my sled. I had a picture of a luge athlete riding a sled. I used that picture to remind me to get back on my sled.

My action step, my habit, was going to be getting back on my sled, after every crash, no matter what. I practiced getting on my sled more than most. I did it when I didn't want to. I did it when it hurt. This was the habit I was going to develop.

Sometimes, after a painful crash, I'd have to work at it. I would have to walk up and down the track for a long time telling reminding myself things like "I'm a winner. I'm going to the Olympics. I never quit. I'm getting back on my sled. When the going gets tough, the tough get going. No matter how bad it gets, I'm going to make it if I don't quit! I never give up!" I thought of that picture of the Olympian on a luge sled. Eventually, I'd get to the point where I could walk up to the coach and say "Coach, I'm ready to get back on my sled."

And it worked. On the road to the Olympics, many athletes much faster than me, much more talented than me, chose to quit along the way. How do you think they felt when they watched the Olympics on TV? The price of getting your dream is big but the pain of regret is hundreds of times bigger.

Create a habit, something you do every day, to develop that quality you need to reach your goal.

You can do it. No matter what your dream is, you can make it happen if you follow these four simple steps: 1) choose a goal, 2) see yourself succeeding,

3) choose a quality, and 4) create a habit to develop your quality. Commit to these four steps.

The difference between people is there are those who are interested in reaching a dream and there are those who are committed to doing whatever it takes to reach their dream. A key to success in life is going from being just interested to being fully committed. Once you are committed you will produce results. At the point of commitment, you mentally "burn all the bridges" and you do whatever it takes to make it happen. That's when you become unstoppable.
Commit to these four steps and you too will make your dreams come true.

What is your goal?

Close your eyes and vividly imagine what it will feel like, taste like, smell like, look like when you realize your goal. **DO IT…NOW!**

What quality do you need to develop to realize your goal?

What new habit will you develop to reach your goal?

The Ultimate Achievement Challenge

The following challenge is for the daring few who are serious about making their goals, dreams, and desires come true. Those afraid to dare might as well stop reading right here. This challenge will weary the lazy because it calls for immediate action. It will bore the sophisticated, and amuse the skeptics.

I don't expect it to be popular because it calls for courage, guts and perseverance. But for a few people reading this book, for the priceless few who decide to go for it, this challenge will result in a renewal of purpose and an exciting, adventurous, exhilarating life.

What I will ask you to do will take you less than 30 minutes a day. Thirty minutes that over a period of time will change the way you think, will create a burning desire for your goals, and will cause you to believe without a shadow of a doubt that you are destined to make your goal a reality.

Once you reach that point, you will be mentally ready to take the journey to your dreams. You will be so mentally strong that you will be absolutely unstoppable. None of the inevitable struggles that you will face will stop you. You will know that you truly are bigger than any circumstances and you will do whatever it takes to make your goals happen.

I challenge you, I dare you to do the following five things seven days a week, 52 weeks a year, for the rest of your life.

Those of you that do will undoubtedly accomplish great things in your lifetimes. Those that don't… well, you know.

Write your goals down every day

Magic happens when you put your goals down on paper. Your subconscious mind starts trying to figure out ways to make your goals become a reality.

Vividly imagine what it will feel like when you reach your goal

Several times a day close your eyes and for a couple of minutes vividly imagine what it's going to feel like when you achieve your goal. This does not have to take up any time. You can do it while you shower. While you're in the elevator. On the way to work. Make it a "Victory Shower" or a "Victory Commute!"

Really get into it. Feel it as if it were really happening. Involve as many of your senses as possible. What will it feel like? What will it taste like? What will it sound like? What will it look like? What will it taste like? Get excited.

Your subconscious does not know the difference between vividly imagining something and it really happening. By doing this, you become passionate about your desire, your belief becomes unshakeable and you become unstoppable.

Success Tip - Get pictures of your goal and put them where you can see them all the time. The walls of my office have always been covered with Olympic flags, posters, mementos, etc. I'm constantly bombarding my brain with where I want to go

Rubber-band your negative self talk away.

This strategy sounds simplistic but if you will do it for 30 days, you will be surprised at how powerful it is. Wear a rubber band around your wrist. Every time you catch yourself saying something negative snap your wrist hard and replace the negative with a positive.

Ex. - Suppose I did something dumb and called myself "Stupid." I'd snap the rubber band and say, "I'm a winner!"

Or suppose I said, "I'll try to do it." I'd snap the rubber band and say, "I'm going to do it!"

What this does is to make you aware of all the negative programming we typically do, nip it in the bud, and replace it with a positive.

Becoming aware of the problem is the first step in correcting it. You will be amazed how much more positive your outlook will become in just 30 days.

Soon you will notice how most people operate from a negative frame of mind and how successful people don't.

Here are some examples of negative and positive phrases:

Negative	Positive
I'm a loser	I'm a winner
I'm failing	I'm learning
This is a problem	This is a challenge
I can't do it	I'll figure it out
I should have	Next time I will
I'll try	I will do it
I can't	I can do it

Read 15 minutes every day
from a positive book

The books you read and the people you associate with will determine where you are in five years. Consistently reading good books will boost your self-belief and will help you to start thinking bigger. You can find a list of some of my favorite books on my website, OlympicMotivation.com.

This does not have to take much time. I keep a book on my bedside table, one in each bathroom, one in my briefcase (you never know when you'll have a few spare minutes), and one in the car (for red lights and traffic jams). I've read some of my books several times. I've read "The Magic of Thinking Big" many, many times. Every time I read it I get something different from it because every time I read it I'm older and ready for new knowledge.

Believe it or not, if all you do is read one book a month, you'll be reading more than 95% of Americans.

If you have teenagers, you might want to reward them whenever they read and write a book report on positive books. Get them thinking success at an early age.

Constantly ask yourself
the winner's question

What's the best thing can I do in the next 15 minutes to get me closer to my goal?

Then do it. Do it right away. Don't kid yourself. Success requires massive action. The first four steps will make you mentally strong so you can consistently and persistently do the fifth step. It's the action that will make your dreams come true.

If you will get in the habit of doing these simple things every day, you will be surprised at how you begin to hit and exceed your goals.

The Courage to Succeed

No matter what your dream is, whether it's to be the best Dad or the best Mom, the best husband or the best wife, the best employee or the best boss, the best salesperson or the best student you can be, to make it a reality, you will have to have the courage to act in spite of your fears.

High achievement requires courage, self-confidence, boldness, and the willingness to go for your goals with no guarantee of success. With courage you can do anything in life. Without it, none of the other qualities will help you.

The first time I saw the Olympics on TV I was in the third grade. As soon as I saw the Olympians I knew I wanted to be just like them. What impressed me the most about the Olympians was not their athletic ability. What I admired about the Olympians was their values. You see, these were people that had a dream, and had the courage to commit fully to it for years with no guarantee of success. That's what impressed me about them.

Sure they had outstanding athletic ability. But more importantly, they had the faith, the guts, the boldness, and the willingness to go for it with no guarantees of success. They had that rare attitude of not worrying about the possibility of failure. They were going to go for it and commit 100% to winning no matter what. It's like they said to themselves, "It's my dream and I'm going for it. That's it period."

When you move boldly towards you goals, when you make the decision to do whatever it takes (and all it is is an attitude change, a choice), magic happens. All of a sudden, unseen forces will come to your aid. The bolder and more committed you are, the more your subconscious will work for you. You will unconsciously start to attract the people and resources you need to achieve your goal. All of a sudden, you will draw energy to making your dream a reality.

Fortune favors the brave. Boldness has magic in it.

People will start saying you are lucky. Winners know there is no such thing as luck. All that is really happening is that now, you have become driven. You are known for your goal. Everybody can see it. Your every action is broadcasting to the world where you are headed, and all of a sudden, anyone who might be interested in helping you, can see you are serious.

When you are focused on your goal, your mind starts acting like a guided missile. It becomes tuned to anything that might help you achieve your goal. This is not any different than when you buy a new car and all of a sudden you notice how many other people are driving the same model car.

When you put all of your energy into one goal, you tap into huge resources. That single decision changes everything. All the stress and worry disappears. Your mental attitude changes completely. You are now the hunter. The dream has become the prey that will eventually succumb to you.

When you make the decision to commit 100%, the winner inside you comes out. The champion inside you comes out. The real you comes out. You just have to have the courage to face your fears.

Your fears are a smokescreen. They are like ghosts that keep you from being the real you. Your best you. It's OK to be afraid. Everyone is afraid.

If everyone is afraid, what's the difference between a brave person and a coward? The brave person acts in spite of his fears. The coward allows his fears to overwhelm him and control his thoughts, feelings and behaviors.

Can courage be developed? Absolutely. Aristotle said, "You become what you repeatedly do." Do you realize the implications of that statement? It means we are not doomed to being the way we currently are. You can change. You can grow. You can be a different person three months from now. In case you haven't figured it out, that excites me. You see, if that is true, and it is, now you know that it is within you to grow into the kind of person that can make your dreams come true.

The way to develop courage is by practicing courage in every situation where courage is required. How do you do that? Through a quality decision.

You come to the realization that whenever you are afraid to do something, you are simply being tested. You make a decision that from now on you will win over your fear. Remember; if you do what you fear, the fear will disappear. If you don't do what you fear, the fear will control your life.

Make a game out of conquering your fears. You can get started with small things. For example, if you usually wait to see what everyone else is having when you're ordering in a restaurant, next time, be the first to order. When you do that, you will have experienced a small personal victory. You just won over that fear.

Next time you are talking to somebody and you want to ask a question but you are afraid of looking stupid, ask anyways. Guess what? You've just won

another personal victory. Score: Fears – 0, Courage
–2.

You need to win many personal victories before you
will win a public victory. Michael Johnson, the 200
meter and 400 meter Olympic Gold medalist, says
in his biography, "I did not miss a scheduled
workout in 10 years." His public victory did not
happen overnight.

Winners develop the courage
to get started and
the courage to endure.

By becoming conscious of your fears and making a
game out of conquering them, before long you will
begin to understand in your heart that fears are just
smokescreens. And by playing that game all the
time, you are becoming more courageous every day.

There are two parts of courage that lead to success.
The first part is the willingness to begin, to act in
faith, to step out boldly in the direction of your
goals with no guarantee of success. The second part
of courage is the willingness to endure, to persist, to
refuse to give up, and to keep on working harder
than anyone else.

Most people talk themselves out of even going for their dream. And most of the ones who make the attempt quit as soon as the going get tough. It's so sad. Because everyone has the ability to make their dreams come true. It's sad that so few people have the willingness to do what it takes.

That's why as a boy I admired the Olympians. That's why we root for the underdog. That's why we love movies like Rocky and Rudy. Because all of us have felt like the underdog at one time or another. Because seeing the underdog win gives us hope that we can win too.

Courage is acting in spite of your fears.

That's why we admire people like speed skater Dan Jansen.

Once you get started on the road to making your dreams a reality, you must make the decision to never quit. The decision to never give up gives you a huge advantage. The person who is most determined usually wins. A study on goals and perseverance found that 95% of the goals that people set are ultimately achieved, as long as the person didn't give up.

Ninety five percent! That's almost a guarantee. A guarantee that if you refuse to quit you will eventually win. The main reason people fail is not because of lack of ability or opportunities. They fail because they lack the inner strength to persist in the face of obstacles and difficulties. That's why trying something almost always leads to failure. By definition, trying something means you will quit if you are not successful.

Don't worry about failing. Failing is how you learn. You can fail over and over again, but all it takes is one big success to wipe out all your previous failures. Just like Dan Jansen in the Lillehammer Olympics. The only time you can't afford to fail is the last time you try.

You need to be bold. Once you have made the decision to never quit, it's easy to be bold. Remember, if you don't quit you're almost guaranteed to succeed. So just assume that success is inevitable. It's only a matter of time. Act as if your ultimate success is guaranteed. No matter how bad it is or how bad it gets, learn from your failures and keep moving on.

Your goal should be to reach the point where you believe in yourself so much that nothing can stop you or hold you back for very long. You want to become unstoppable. This is where persistence is so important. The more you persist, the more you will believe in yourself. And the more you believe in yourself, the more you persist. Your persistence is a measure of how much you believe in yourself and how much you believe in your ability to succeed.

If you act as if you are guaranteed to succeed, your belief will grow. Because emotion follows motion. What you do determines how we will feel. Act in spite of your fears and commit to not quit, and I'll promise you that the winner inside you will burst forth to propel you to victory.

When you develop your courage and perseverance, you will experience life in ways you never thought were possible. The more you practice courage and perseverance, the more confident you will become. Don't quit. Refuse to quit and you will succeed. Dan Jansen refused to quit and look at what happened...

Dan Jansen was supposed to win gold in the Sarajevo 84 Olympics. He didn't. Disappointed, he knew he should bring home a medal in the 88 Calgary games. But only moments before the start of the race he was told his sister, Jane had died of leukemia. With this weighing on his mind, he raced poorly and walked home empty handed. Dan had another chance in Nagano 92, but his hopes were crushed again when he slipped on the ice. The 94 Lillehammer would be his last chance.

With the world holding its breath as he raced in the 500 meters, he fell again to the horror of the crowd, and finished eighth. With only one race left in his career, the 1000 meters, Dan Jansen was racing for his life. Incredibly he slipped on the last turn…but didn't fall. As he raced past the finish line, he read the official time. A new world record. At long last Dan Jansen's perseverance paid off. Finally he had won the Olympic Gold Medal. On his victory lap, he carried his baby daughter on his shoulders. Her name is Jane… after his sister.

Do the things you fear, or else fear will control your life.

Dan's story is so inspirational. It makes us feel like we can't fail. It teaches us lessons in courage and perseverance. It has been said, "The Honor should not go to those who have not fallen; rather, all Honor should go to those who fall and rise again." That's why we love Rocky, and Rudy, and the Olympics.

The Olympics are not really about sports. The Olympics are about the power of the human spirit. They are a place that showcases to the world a group of people that were willing to go after their dreams no matter what.

The Olympic flame represents the fire in the heart

of someone who is in pursuit of their dream. At the 2002 Salt Lake City Olympics Opening Ceremonies, Mitt Romney, the CEO of the Olympic Organizing Committee faced all of the athletes and said to us, "Athletes, you are proof to the world that when you have a dream, and you pursue it, and you refuse to quit, dreams do come true. After the Olympics it is your responsibility to teach that philosophy to others. Teach them how to make their dreams come true. And let's make this world a better place."

So have the courage to go after your dream. Give it all you've got. Have the courage to get started and have the courage to never quit. I guarantee you, when you do, your life will become great.

Are you willing to step out on faith, jump into the arena, and fight for your dream?

Once you start the fight, are you willing to do whatever it takes to get the job done?

You will only realize your dream if you have the courage to get going and the courage to persist. Do you?

If you're not sure, who are the most encouraging people you know? Who are the people who will not let you quit? Will you become accountable to them?

How To Get Yourself To Take Action

How do you find the consistency to keep doing what you know you need to do day after day after day after day? I've struggled with that issue all my life. How do I get myself to consistently do what I know I need to be doing?

Like anything else, it's all a mental game. And the best way to win the mental battle is by using everything in your arsenal at once. To do a variety of things to get you to perform like you know you should.

I use all of the following techniques...

 - Focus on the dream. Focus on what drives me to take action.

 - Write the goal down and read it daily.

 - Constantly visualize how great it will feel when I reach my goal (to get my desire for gain working for me).

 - Visualize how awful it will feel if I don't reach my goal (to get my fear of loss working for me).

 - Using positive affirmations whenever a negative

thought enters my mind.

 - Sharing my goal with people who support me to build pressure.

Doing all of this is simple but not easy. But it works.

I will illustrate all six techniques by telling you what I'm doing to get myself back into "fighting weight."

It all goes back to the dream. It all goes back to your "Why?" It all comes back to having a burning desire that drives you to consistently and persistently do what you need to do.

You need to figure out what drives you. Then you have to develop a burning desire. Your focus should not be on the process. Your focus needs to be on the dream.

When I was training for the Olympics it was a lot easier for me to eat right and to be in the gym six days a week. The Olympic dream was so powerful that it got me to do whatever it took to get the job done.

In order to keep myself driven I used both positive and negative motivation. I constantly visualized how good it was going to feel when I made my

Olympic dream a reality, and I visualized how awful it would be if I didn't make it.

Sometimes what drove me to go to the gym was the thought that if I didn't, there was going to be some German competitor hitting the gym today and I didn't want him to get ahead of me.

After the Salt Lake City Olympics, there was no longer any driving force to get me to go to the gym. There was no driving force to get me to eat right. Consequently, in no time I put on a lot of weight. I just could not get myself motivated to go to the gym.

In fact, I started coming up with great reasons not to go. I rationalized not working out by telling myself that I needed that time to work on building my speaking business. I was working very long days, but that was no excuse. I had become sedentary, and not only did I not reduce my caloric intake, I probably increased it.

I tried all kind of things to get myself to watch my weight but I did not stick with anything because there was no driving force.

Finally, I realized that I had been focusing on the process without a dream. I needed to tie a huge reward and a huge penalty to losing or not losing X amount of weight by a certain date.

Remember, your goals need to have a date to create urgency. And they need to be written down and read daily.

I love to travel. And my family was due for a vacation. So I tied losing weight to a family vacation.

All of a sudden, the pressure was on. My new focus was on the vacation.

The willingness to act – to overcome inertia – is the first step on the path to greatness.

I also changed my mindset on how going to the gym affected my business. I came to the realization that I have a lot more energy when I'm working out. Believe it or not, after working out, my body is energized for 3-4 hours. Plus I'm more mentally alert. The ideal would be to work our early in the morning, and go out for a jog or a bike ride at lunch to get energized for the afternoon.

So I changed my perspective. Instead of looking at it as time lost, I started looking at working out as a way to get me to work at a peak level.

Another technique I used was saying positive affirmations to push my food thoughts away. Every time I think about food I say, "I'm a lean, mean, fighting machine!"

I'm fighting for my dreams.

Believe me, It works. The other night I was at a bookstore and I noticed that somehow I had wound up in the "Cookbooks" section. It's like I'm being tested. I was actually leafing through a cookbook dreaming away before I realized what I was doing. I put the cookbook down and said my new mantra, "I'm a lean, mean, fighting machine!" and got out of that section as fast as I could.

Another day, while driving through town, I passed a bunch of restaurants. The whole time I was wearing my new phrase out. "I'm a lean, mean fighting machine!"

Another thing you want to do is to put some pressure on yourself by telling others about your goal.

So fight it on all fronts. Develop the habit of controlling your thoughts or else your thoughts will control you.

What do you want to accomplish?

How badly do you want it?

Are you willing to put yourself on the line by telling others about your goal?

No Guts No Glory

You know in your heart what you'd like to accomplish. You're always thinking about it. It bugs you all the time. Just the thought of doing it makes your skin tingle.

The thought of finally making that dream a reality makes you feel alive, excited, pumped up with a terrific feeling of anticipation.

But something is holding you back. What if you go for it and you fail? How could you live with yourself? What would others think?

Fear of failure holds most people back from going after their dreams. Every day you hesitate, the fear grows stronger.

The fear is just a smokescreen. I dare you to act in spite of your fears. You'll be so glad you did. Regardless of the results, you will feel so proud of yourself. And even if you do fail (which really means you need to keep trying until you figure out how to succeed), others will look up to you for having the guts to act with courage.

Go for it. Just going for it will put you in the top 5% of the population. Why? Because 95% of the people out there are afraid to go for it.

The one quality that separates the most successful people from the least is initiative. Initiative means taking responsibility and taking action when you see something needs to be done. It means moving quickly and decisively.

Whatever you sincerely desire, act as if it were impossible to fail, and it shall be.

Initiative means taking risks, regularly moving out of the comfort zone, doing things the average person is not willing to do. You can do it. You have it in you. You really do. I know. I know because I'm an average person that accomplished great things only because I am willing to constantly dive headfirst out of my comfort zone.

Believe me, when you do, the world will conspire to help your dreams become a reality.

Do you have the guts to go for it?

Imagine how dreadful your life will be if you don't go for your dream…

Imagine what an adventure your life will be if you dedicate it to the pursuit of your dreams….

When your grandchildren ask you what you did with your life, will you tell them you played it safe or will you enthrall them with the stories of your adventures?

What do you want the people at your funeral to say about you?

Go for it. You'll be glad you did.

Take a Chance

The most successful people in the world are risk takers. As soon as the see an opportunity, they move quickly and make something happen. They have a special quality that sets them apart from less successful people. They take initiative in everything they do.

Successful people accept responsibility and take action when they see something needs to be done. They move quickly. They don't suffer from paralysis of analysis. They just do something. Anything that will get them closer to their goal.

By taking action - massive action - they build momentum and soon good things start to happen. One of my business mentors likes to say, "Most people need to think less and act more." Another of my mentors always says, "Done is better than perfect." Another way to say it is – implement now, perfect later.

If you want to succeed, be willing to fail. To succeed big, be willing to fail big. To succeed fast, be willing to fail fast.

Successful people are willing to try different approaches to reach their goal. They are not worried about failing. They are just focused on the result. They just throw mud on the wall knowing that if they throw enough, some of it will stick.

They never focus on the approaches that didn't work. There's no time for that. Wallowing with self pity is for losers. Winners simply learn from their mistakes and quickly try a different approach.

Dream as if you'll live forever. Live as if you'll die today.

The faster they move, the more energy they have. The more different things they try, the more likely they are of succeeding. They make a game out of it. And they never take their focus away from the goal. Their attitude is – there is always a way. I will find a way. I will succeed.

A national survey of octogenarians revealed that their biggest regret in life was not having had taken enough risks. Think about that. What they're saying is they realize they did not live life to the fullest and they missed out. When you turn eighty you don't want to have that regret. So go for it. Take a chance. Do something. You'll be glad you did.

Are you going to go for it or not? If you're not, why don't you just give this book to someone who will use it?

Are you mad yet? I hope so. Most people don't do anything until they get mad. Use your anger to chase your dream. Passion is positive anger.

Stop analyzing everything. Think less and act more. You are worthy of your dream.

What's holding you back? I guarantee you that it's just a smokescreen. Go for it. You'll be glad you did.

Focus - You Won't Succeed Without It

Being focused is not an option if you are serious about realizing your dreams. Being focused on your dream is critical to making it become a reality.

Back in 1984, when I made a decision to take up the sport of luge and make a run at the Olympics, I took an 8x10 photo of a luge racer and hung it up across from my bed.

The first thing I saw every morning was "The Luge Man." He reminded me to work out, eat right and surround myself with winners.

The last thing I saw every night before I turned off the lights was "The Luge Man." All night long I would dream about the luge and about the Olympics.

I never met "The Luge Man," but he is one of my heroes. He helped keep me focused on my objective. And he was a factor that helped make my dream come true.

Here's a great story of someone else whose dream was focused by a photograph...

The Great Depression was not kind to legendary hotelier Conrad Hilton. After the crash of 1929, people weren't traveling, and if they were, they weren't staying in the hotels Hilton had acquired during the boom years of the 1920s.

Your ability to single-mindedly focus on your top priorities will determine how much you accomplish.

By 1931, his creditors were threatening to foreclose, his laundry was in hock, and he was borrowing money from a bellboy so he could eat. That year, Hilton came across a photograph of the Waldorf Hotel with its six kitchens, 200 cooks, 500 waiters, 2000 rooms, and its private hospital and private railroad siding in the basement. Hilton clipped the photograph out of the magazine and wrote across it, "The Greatest of Them All."

The year 1931 was "a presumptuous, an outrageous time to dream," Hilton later wrote. But he put the photo of the Waldorf in his wallet, and when he had a desk again, slipped the picture under the glass top. From then on it was always in front of him. As he worked his way back up and acquired new bigger desks, he would slip the cherished photo under the glass. Eighteen years later, in October 1949, Conrad Hilton acquired the Waldorf.

That picture gave Hilton's dream shape and substance. There was something for his mind to focus upon. It became a cue for his behavior.

How focused are you on achieving your goal? Is it an obsession?

Do you write your goal every day? You need to. Writing your goal daily is an act of commitment that slowly turns you into a guided missile that can't miss.

Do you surround yourself with pictures of your goal? If your goal is to drive a Ferrari, do you regularly test-drive Ferraris? Do you subscribe to Ferrari Magazine? You need to.

Birds of a Feather

Who you surround yourself with will determine how far you go.

After I decided to take up the sport of luge and train for the 1988 Calgary Winter Olympics, decision making became pretty simple for me. I knew that every action I took in the next four years was either going to get me closer to my goal or pull me away from my goal. Everything I did would make a difference. Even the people I associated with would make a difference.

You see, there are two kinds of people in the world. They are either on your team or they are not in your team. They are either on your dream team or they are not. People will either encourage you or cast doubt. If they doubt you can do it, they could steal your dream away.

Associating with negative people makes us think negatively. Close contact with petty individuals develops petty habits in us. On the other hand, companionship with people with big ideas raises the level of our thinking; close contact with ambitious people helps make us more ambitious.

I came to the realization that if someone laughed at my dream; they were laughing at me. If they did not believe in me, I stopped associating with them. I had to. They had the power to make me doubt myself and ultimately quit.

I was taking up the luge at the age of 21 - way too old. And I was trying to qualify for the Olympics just four years away. I could not leave anything to chance. I did not have time to waste. I needed to know right away who was for me and who was not.

If you fly with eagles, you will think, feel and act like an eagle.

How did I do it? I told everyone I spoke with about my dream. If they laughed at me, rolled their eyes, or in any way showed lack of belief, I stopped associating with them. I could not afford to. They were a dream stealer. However, if they got excited about my dream, I held on to them like they were made out of Gold. I'd just found myself a cheerleader.

By doing this all the time, before long I could have filled a cheering section with my supporters. An unexpected benefit of doing this was that I created a positive pressure that kept me from quitting when the going got tough. You see, no matter how rough a day I was having at the track, it was going to be easier to get back on the sled than to come back home and tell everyone that I had quit.

Birds of a feather flock together. Make sure you're in the right flock. It's your choice.

Who are you spending most of your time with?

Are you spending your time with the people that will lead you to your dream?

Are you associating with people who encourage you and push you to take greater risks?

Or are you hanging around with people who are keeping you where you are? Remember, ninety percent of success is a result of who you hang around with.

How I Turned Singles Luge Into a Team Sport

When I decided to take up the luge and train for the Olympics I was 21 years old. Back then I thought I could make it to the Olympics all by myself. I still had a lot of growing up to do.

In "Seven Habits of Highly Effective People," Steven Covey talks about three stages people go through - dependence, independence, and interdependence. At 21, I was still in the independent stage and needed to move on to becoming interdependent.

Along the way I realized that I needed some help. In order to accomplish great things I was going to have to develop some leadership and people skills to build a team. Then I would have to work through the team to make my Olympic dream come true. I was going to have to turn singles luge into a team sport.

It's no different in any big project or endeavor. Lone Rangers never accomplish as much as people who work through teams.

I like to keep things simple. I believe it takes only two things to be a good leader. It takes passion and integrity.

If you are passionate about your mission, you will attract the people who are like minded; people who would like to be a part of your mission. I was passionate. I told everyone I talked to about my Olympic dream. Everyone. And I was excited about it. I was not wishy-washy. Other people had no doubt that I believed in and was committed to the dream.

You need to work through other people to accomplish great things.

By doing that, whenever I talked to someone who was interested in the Olympics, I became their link to the Olympic Games. And many times they were willing to help me out.

Believe me; I needed a lot of help.

I needed financial help. It's very expensive to be flying all over the world to train and compete. You're also out of work for months at a time. Everyone thinks I have corporate sponsors. People ask me, "Ruben, who are your sponsors? Coke? Pepsi? Nike?" My sponsors were Visa and MasterCard baby! I charged everything on my cards. And after maxing out my credit cards, my family lent me tens of thousands of dollars. It's part of the price you pay to succeed.

I needed medical help. Doctors, Chiropractors, and massage therapists that kept me healthy and patched me up after bad crashes.

Finally, I needed spiritual help. I needed people who would keep my spirits up when I was struggling. Especially in the beginning. People who would keep me from quitting. The first year I was crashing four out of five times. It got to the point where even after crashing, it was going to be easier to get back on the sled than to come home and tell everyone I had quit. I couldn't quit. I didn't want to let the team down.

To build a Dream Team, you must dream big, be passionate, and be a person of high integrity and character.

My passion about the Olympic dream attracted people to me. I believe everyone has the capacity to be passionate about something. Unfortunately, most people keep their passion all bottled in. They don't want to show their passion out of fear of what others might think. I didn't care what others thought. I actually wanted to know who did not believe in me so I could stop associating with them.

I made it a point to only spend time with my supporters. Doing so made me unstoppable.

The first part of leadership is passion for the cause. The second part is integrity.

Would you follow someone you don't trust? Of course not. So if you want to be the leader and have others follow you, you need to be absolutely trustworthy. Your word is Gold. You keep your word. You start being very careful about what you promise. You must deliver on every promise. Every time you don't, your credibility and your reputation will suffer.

If you have passion for the cause and you are a person of integrity, you'll be ahead of 95% of the people out there. People will be attracted to you, and you will be able to accomplish great things.

Have you been trying to do everything by yourself?

Who are three key people that could help you massively accelerate your progress?

What's keeping you from enlisting them to your cause?

When people think about you, do they associate you with your dream? If not, you probably need to be more passionate about your dream.

Bouncing Back Quickly
to Win

You've probably never heard of him. In Hungary, he's a national hero. Everybody in Hungary knows his name and his incredible story. After reading his story, you'll never forget him...

Back in 1938, Karoly Takacs of the Hungarian Army, was the top pistol shooter in the world. He was expected to win the gold in the 1940 Olympic Games scheduled for Tokyo.

Those expectations vanished one terrible day just months before the Olympics. While training on military maneuvers with his squad, a hand grenade exploded in Takacs' right hand. Takacs' shooting hand was blown off.

Takacs spent a month in the hospital depressed at both the loss of his hand, and the end to his Olympic dream. At that point most people would have quit. And they would have probably spent the rest of their life feeling sorry for themselves. Takacs was a winner though. Winners know that they can't let circumstances keep them down. They understand that life is hard and that they can't let life beat them down. Winners know in their heart that quitting is not an option.

Takacs did the unthinkable; he picked himself up, dusted himself off, and decided to learn how to shoot with his left hand. His reasoning was simple. He simply asked himself, "Why not?"

Instead of focusing on what he didn't have – a world class right shooting hand, he decided to focus on what he did have – incredible mental toughness, and a healthy left hand he could develop to shoot like a champion.

Takacs practiced by himself. No one knew what he was doing. Maybe he didn't want to subject himself to people who most certainly would have discouraged him from his rekindled dream. In the spring of 1939 he showed up at the Hungarian National Pistol Shooting Championship.

Other shooters approached Takacs to give him their condolences and to congratulate him on having the strength to come watch them shoot. They were surprised when he said, "I didn't come to watch, I came to compete." They were even more surprised when Takacs won.

The 1940 and 1944 Olympics were cancelled because of World War II. It looked like Takacs' Olympic Dream would never have a chance to realize itself. But Takacs kept training and in 1944 he qualified for the London Olympics. At the age of

38, Takacs won the Gold Medal and set a new world record in pistol shooting. Four years later, Takacs won the Gold Medal at the 1952 Helsinki Olympics. Takacs was a man with the mental toughness to bounce back from anything.

Winners in every field have a special trait that helps them become unstoppable. A special characteristic that allows them to survive major setbacks on the road to success. Winners recover quickly. Bouncing back is not enough. Winners bounce back quickly. They take their hit, they experience their setback, they have the wind taken out of their sails, but they immediately recover. Right away they force themselves to look at the bright side of things – *any* bright side, and they say to themselves, "That's OK. There is always a way. I will find a way." They dust themselves off, and pick up where they left off.

The reason quick recovery is important is that if you recover quickly, you don't lose your momentum and your drive. Takacs recovered in only one month. If he had wallowed in his misery, if he had stayed "under the circumstances," if he had played the martyr, and felt sorry for himself much longer, he would have lost his mental edge – his "eye of the tiger" and he never would have been able to come back.

When a boxer gets knocked down, he has ten seconds to get back up. If he gets up in eleven seconds, he loses the fight. Remember that next time you get knocked down.

Takacs definitely had a right to feel sorry for himself. He had a right to stay depressed and to ask himself "Why me?" for the rest of his life. He had the right to act like a mediocre man. He even had the right to let his terrible accident cause him to take up heavy drinking, to quit on life altogether, and to end his life. He had the right to act like a loser.

But Takacs made the decision to dig deep inside and to find a solution. To pick himself up and to learn to shoot all over again. Winners always search for a solution. Losers always search for an escape.

Next time you get knocked down, act like a winner. Act like Takacs. Get up quickly, and astound the world.

When life hits you with adversity, do you wallow in your misery? Or do you instantly look for ways to bounce back?

When you have challenges, do you waste time whining and complaining to people that could not possibly help you? Or do you seek people that have overcome those challenges?

Next time life knocks you down, pretend you are a boxer that must do whatever it takes to get back up in 10 seconds…or else. Focus on how you can get back up. Because the longer you're down, the harder it will be to regain your momentum.

What's Holding You Back?

Whether your dream is to lose weight, or to buy
your dream home, or to double your income, or to
learn the ins and outs of soccer so you can coach
your daughter's soccer team, you will find that there
are things that hold you back.

Ninety five percent of people, look at their obstacles
and all they see is a reason why they can't make
their dream a reality. They look at the obstacle, get
discouraged, they lose heart, and they quit. Winners
look at the obstacles, get mad and then become
determined to overcome them.

When I decided to take up the sport of luge and
train for the Olympics four years away, I knew I had
two major obstacles to overcome. Two things that
had to happen or else I would be watching the
Olympics on TV: first, I had to be ranked in the top
50 lugers in the world to qualify. In order for that to
happen, I would only have only two luge seasons to
learn how to slide, because the last two seasons I
needed to race internationally to work on my world
ranking.

If you really want to know how I was able to do it,
the rest of that story is in my book, "The Courage to
Succeed."

What's more important than the rest of the story is how you can develop the mental toughness to look at an obstacle and become fired up and excited about the challenge ahead.

Many times all you have to do to overcome your roadblocks is to simply learn some new skills. Other times, you might have to refine some skills. You might have to enlist the help of other people. I did. Big time. You might have to create a team. Most of the time the roadblock is internal – lack of belief and doubt that you can pull it off.

The roadblocks are not a bad thing. They are simply road signs that tell you what you need to work on next. Where your focus needs to be. Your roadblocks help define what your goals need to be.

What's keeping you from realizing your dreams? What's the one thing that's slowing down all your progress? Your job is to identify the roadblocks and focus all your energy on doing whatever it takes to remove them. Once you do that, your dreams will be there for the taking.

What are the three top things that are keeping you from your dream?

What can you do today to overcome those challenges?

Who do you know that has had and has overcome those challenges?

Call them up, take them out for coffee, and find out how they did it – they'll be glad to help. Successful people like to talk about their success.

Walking Your Talk

Leaders in every field agree that there is a shortage of people who get things done. People who get results. That is great news. It's an opportunity for all of us. What that means is that if you want to move up in your field, all you have to do is to start getting results.

So how do you do that? By becoming a person of action. Massive action.

Having good ideas is not enough. Even having great ideas is not enough. Ideas are a dime a dozen. However, people that implement ideas are priceless. Everything that exists in this world is the product of an idea that was acted upon. Even the chair you're sitting in.

Successful people are active. They get it done. They don't waste any time. They have an urgency about them. Passive people are not successful. Passive people procrastinate. Put things off. They wait for everything to be perfect before acting.

Well, I have news for you. Conditions have never been or never will be perfect. What if Eisenhower had waited until conditions were perfect to invade Normandy? What if Kennedy had waited until conditions were perfect before deciding to put a man on the moon? What if Columbus had waited for conditions were perfect before setting out on his voyage?

When you are about to take a family vacation you probably don't wait until all the lights are green. You get started, and you handle the red lights as you come across them. Use that approach with everything else.

Commitment creates opportunity. Stop talking and start doing.

Do something. Get started. Move. Get some momentum going. If you don't, you'll regret it and you will be filled with stress. Stress comes from not doing what you know you should be doing.

Once you get started, once you are in motion, your mind starts focusing on how to get the job done. As soon as you get in motion you move ahead of the competition – all those poor souls that are still "thinking about it."

Action produces confidence. Inaction strengthens fear. Just think about when you were a kid on the high dive in your neighborhood pool. The longer you waited to dive, the worse the fear got. But once you decided to dive, the fear was gone and you spent the rest of the afternoon diving. Taking action made it fun. Exhilarating.

You know what you need to do. Do it now. Get going. Get started. Become an action fanatic. You'll be glad you did.

If you're not willing to take action, do us all a favor and **STOP TALKING ABOUT IT!**

What's the one thing you can do in the next 15 minutes that will propel your dream forward?

Why aren't you doing it?

Your new mantra needs to be "Do It Now!" "Do It Now!" "Do It Now!"

The Power to Choose

In his book "Roots," Alex Haley tells about something unexpected that happened right after slavery was abolished. The newly freed slaves did not know how to be free. All their lives they had had others make their decisions for them, consequently, they had never learned how to make choices.

You could say their "choice-making muscles" needed developing. Many of the slaves actually stayed with their masters and worked for them for the rest of their lives.

In the movie "The Shawshank Redemption," when Brooks, the prison librarian, who's been an inmate for 50 years, is set free, he does not know how to be a free man. He does not know how to use his power to choose. All his life he has been told what to do. For Brooks, life as a free man is so overwhelming, that he ends up committing suicide (life's worst choice).

Most people's "choice-making muscles" could use a little strengthening. After all, when we are young, our parents and our teachers tell us what to do. Then we get a job and our boss tells us what to do.

We start drifting through life instead of designing our future. We start existing instead of living. And we end up using a fraction of our gifts. We forget that we have the power to choose who we want to be, what we want to accomplish, where we want to live, etc. We stop taking responsibility for our results, and start living as a victim, instead of as a victor.

You are the master of your fate. You are the Captain of your soul.

You and I have the power to choose what we do with our lives. You are where you are because of the choices you've made. If you don't like where you are, you need to start making different choices. I've been in sales all my life. Whenever I've ever had a slow sales month, I could always trace it to lack of activity a few months back.

Likewise, whenever my pants start feeling tight around the waist, I can always trace it to having been overeating recently. It's not rocket science.

My Dad always told me, "It's not what happens to you, it's how you handle it." He also said to me, "You have the power to choose your destiny." It wasn't until I started acting like I believed those things that my life started getting interesting.
I have a little secret for you. There is a magical

moment between your circumstances and your results. That moment is called *choice*.

When something happens to you, when circumstances happen to you, when things that seem unfair happen to you, don't whine and complain. The instant you start blaming your circumstances is the instant you become a victim. Once you do that, you can kiss your future goodbye. Remember, you can choose your response to those circumstances.

Make a wise choice, handle it properly, and watch your results improve tremendously. What kind of life do you want? The good news is that you have the power to create it.

Once you stop making excuses and start taking responsibility for your results, your life will start getting really exciting. It did for me.

Have you been making excuses? Don't you realize that everyone has challenges? Don't you realize that making excuses is what losers do?

Stop making excuses. Whenever a winner hears you making an excuse, they want to get as far away from you as possible. Resolve to do something right now about what's holding you back. Resolve to become an inspiration to others who share your challenges.

You're Only Six Inches Away

Back when I took up the sport of luge, one of my Olympic coaches used to tell me, "Ruben, you're only six inches away from massive success." I wasn't sure what he meant. He explained, "Six inches is the distance between your ears. Your success depends on what you feed your mind." He was talking about the "Inner Game." It would be years before I really understood what he meant. Today, I realize that he was 100% right.

You always hear about the mental part of sports being more important than the physical part. I have to admit that I was always a bit skeptical. I was skeptical until a cold morning in October 1998.

I took up the sport of luge in 1984 and I retired from the luge right after the 1992 Albertville Olympics. After Albertville, I didn't take a luge run for six years.

However, during those six years I read hundreds of books on success and listened to thousands of motivational tapes. I didn't realize it, but by doing that, I was becoming mentally tougher.

In 1998, six years after retiring from the luge, I decided to begin training for the 2002 Salt Lake

City Olympics.

My first day of training was unforgettable. I was at the start of the Calgary luge track ready to take my first run in six years. Surprisingly, I was feeling cool, calm, and confident. Believe it or not, my first four runs were personal bests. I felt I had more control of the sled than ever before. Four personal bests after a six year break. Unbelievable! That day I stopped being a skeptic. That day I became a believer in the power of the human mind.

Success requires massive action. The key is getting yourself to take action.

Olympic athletes use several mental training techniques to sharpen their competitive edge - techniques designed to keep them hungry, confident, and mentally tough so they will do what it takes to win - techniques anyone can use to get better results in their personal or professional life.

One thing we all do is read our goals on a daily basis. We write our goals as a series of positive affirmations that help program ourselves for success.

We also use subliminal techniques. The walls of my office are covered with Olympic memorabilia. I surround myself with pictures which constantly bombard my mind with where I want to go. Doing this helps me become unstoppable on the way to my goals.

Top achievers in every field are always on the lookout for anything that will give them an edge on the competition.

Success doesn't just happen. Success requires massive action. Thomas Edison said, "Genius is 2% inspiration and 98% perspiration." The key to success in anything is getting ourselves to take consistent and persistent action.

What do you want to accomplish? Better sales? A promotion at work? Better grades? How bad do you want it? Do you want it badly enough to get the tools that will help program yourself to take action?

Remember, you're only six inches away.

The Champion's Creed

Back when I was in grade school I was pretty shy and timid. Reading biographies revealed to me that courage was a major factor in success. From that point on I read everything I could get my hands on how people developed courage. I read about warriors, and people that overcame great odds.

One day I was reading an old out-of-print book about English knights. There was a poem that the knights read before going to battle. A poem that gave them strength and courage.

The poem was hard to understand because it was written in Old English. I took my favorite lines of the poem and re-wrote them in modern English. Over the years whenever I've come across a powerful affirmation, I've added it to my list.

The affirmation is called **"The Champion's Creed."** I've been reading it daily for years and it's helped me develop mental toughness.

I've taken this affirmation with me all over the world. Reading it regularly helps me become unstoppable. It's like putting on mental armor.

The best way to use this is to take it with you to a mirror (preferably one where you are standing up to see yourself) and read it with power and conviction while looking right at the reflection of your eyes.

You'll be amazed at the difference the mirror makes.

The Champion's Creed

I am a champion.

I believe in myself.

I have the will to win.

I set high goals for myself.

I surround myself with winners.

I'm cool, positive, and confident.

I'm willing to pay the price of success.

I love the struggle and competition.

I stay relaxed and in control at all times.

I focus all my energy on the job at hand.

I vividly imagine what victory will feel like.

I am a champion and I <u>will</u> win.

For your FREE printable color copy of
The Champion's Creed visit…

TheChampionsCreed.com

Success Secrets of a Four-Time Olympian

You are a lot closer to success than you realize.

What I'm saying is you are designed with all the resources needed to make your fondest dreams come true. You only need to learn how to condition your mind for success. Ninety percent of the input you get in the world is negative. And most of the things you tell yourself are probably negative. So it is critical to learn techniques to replace the negative with positive.

In life you don't get what you want. You get what you are. The best way to improve yourself is to change what goes into your mind. You are a product of what goes into your mind. What you think determines what you do. What you do determines what you accomplish.

Olympic Athletes understand this. We know that what goes into our mind will ultimately determine how well we do in our competition. Think of each thought as a computer "bit," the smallest unit of information possible. Many thoughts add up to become beliefs. What we believe determines how high we will go. The good news is there are ways to raise your belief level.

Beliefs are extremely important. For example, in April 1954, the belief in the world was that it was impossible to run the mile in less than four minutes.

Then along came Roger Bannister. Bannister did what nobody in the history of the world had ever done. He broke the four-minute mile barrier. The phenomenal thing is that later the same month, several other athletes did it too. And since then, over 20,000 people have run the mile in under four minutes.

There are ways to increase your belief level.

What changed? The BELIEF changed. All of a sudden athletes knew "If Roger can do it so can I."

Most people never attempt to do something they don't believe they can do.

Ever since I was in the third grade I wanted to be an Olympic Athlete. But it was not until I was in college and saw Scott Hamilton compete in the Sarajevo games that I made a decision to train for the Olympics.

How did I raise my self-belief level between third grade and college? Two ways - through the books I read and through the people I associated with.

I read countless biographies of great people. Before long, I realized that the common denominator in the success of those great people was the fact they had a dream they were passionate about and they never gave up.

Perseverance is the best trait you can have. But how do you keep yourself going when the going gets tough? It comes back to your beliefs.

The other thing I did to raise my self-esteem was to regularly associate with people I respected. When you hang around people that think big, you start to think big. And when people you have respect for believe in you, you start to believe in yourself.

Four years after making a decision to begin training for the Olympics, I had the honor of competing in the 1988 Calgary Winter Olympics in the luge.

How does someone who did not even take up the sport of luge until he was 22 become a Four-Time Olympian? As I tell thousands of people in my speeches, I'm not a big shot. I'm just a little shot that keeps on shooting. I'm proof that ordinary people can accomplish extraordinary things if they will just put the right things into their minds.

Olympic Athletes consistently and persistently use specialized techniques to program their minds to achieve peak performance. The following simple

techniques performed consistently over a period of
time will change your outlook in life and ultimately
your outcomes.

Visualize the Desired Outcome.

Several times a day close your eyes and for a couple
of minutes vividly imagine what it's going to feel
like when you achieve your goal. Really get into it.
Feel it as if it were really happening. Get excited.

Your subconscious does not know the difference
between imagining it and it really happening. By
doing this, you become passionate about your
desire, your belief becomes unshakeable and you
become unstoppable.

The luge team is taught to visualize their sled runs
every day. Especially right before practice. We "run
the mental tape" in our minds of each twist, turn and
body movement so when we're hurling down the
track at 80+ MPH, we instinctively know what to
do in all situations.

I constantly visualized what it was going to be like
when I walked into the Olympic Stadium at the
Opening Ceremonies. I could see the crowds
waving at me. I could see the flags and the balloons.
I could hear the roar of the crowd, the fireworks, the
Olympic Hymn. I could feel the cold wind blowing
snow onto my cheeks. I could feel the tears of joy

streaming down my face. I could feel the goose bumps running up my back and over my shoulders.

I thought about it all the time, even while jogging, while lifting weights, in the shower, etc. It was my dream. And when I finally entered the Olympic arena, it was just the same only 100 times better.

Find a Mentor or a Coach

The "Why" is always more important than the "How." Don't worry how you will make your dream come true. The dream gives you the energy. Find someone who has already been successful in doing what you want to do, not just someone who talks the talk.

Ask them to be your mentor and teach you how to be successful as they are. If you are serious and committed to achieving your dream, they will see the passion in your eyes and will be honored to be asked.

As soon as I decided to take up the luge and train for the Calgary Olympics, I contacted the U.S. Luge Association in Lake Placid, NY. I asked the USLA if they would teach me how to luge and prepare me for the Olympics four years away. They said they had a plan in place and that if I would follow the plan and not quit, I would have a chance of making it. Without knowing what the plan was, I humbled myself to my new mentors and let them know I would do whatever they said I needed to do.

That is the ideal mentor-mentee relationship. A hungry, driven, eager to learn, yet humble mentee together with a giving, knowledgeable, successful mentor.

Setting goals, visualizing the desired outcome, and finding a mentor are basic yet critical steps to succeeding in life. Every Olympic athlete I've ever met does all three consistently. It's just a decision. By consistently and persistently following these steps, you will reach your goals and dreams faster than 95% of the people in the world.

Chase your dreams, go for the gold, and never, ever give up.

Dream, Struggle, Victory

Back when I was in grade school, my dad encouraged me to study the lives of successful people. He said, "Success leaves clues. Read biographies and you'll figure out what works in life."

I've been a student of success ever since. I've read countless biographies and I've found them all to be very similar. They are all the story of someone that had a dream, faced a struggle, and finally had a victory. Dream, struggle, victory.

The struggle is what makes you strong.

We all have dreams. What made those people different is they had the guts to take action. The dream was a call to action – an inner longing to strike out on an adventure. They chose to heed the call and take the journey.

Choosing to take the journey takes courage. And staying the course to victory takes courage and perseverance. That's why we admire people who go for it. Because they have the heart of a champion and the adventurous spirit of winners.

Something life-changing happens when you decide to take the journey. If you refuse to quit, you will inevitably find you have hidden resources and abilities within you. You find out what you're made of.

You always win by taking the journey. The journey transforms you. Who you become is the true purpose of the journey.

Face your fear. Take the journey. Heed the call. Bite off more than you think you can chew. Do it now. You'll never be the same.

179 Tips to Make This Your Best Year Ever

Count your blessings daily.
Doing so will keep you in a positive state of mind.

Surround yourself with positive, encouraging,
successful people. They will pull you up
no matter what the circumstances.

Come to terms with the fact that in life
there is no free lunch.

It's not what happens to you,
it's how you handle it.

Deliver more than you are paid to.
Make yourself indispensable to others.

Focus on your strengths. Find an arena
you are suited to play in, have the courage
to get started, have the courage to not quit,
and decide you will give it all you've got
for as long as it takes to get the job done.

Live this day as if it were your last.
Treat others as if it were *their* last day.

Take your projects seriously
but learn to laugh at yourself.

Don't neglect the details. Excellence comes
from taking care of the details.

Smile more. It makes you more approachable,
and makes it easier to build your dream team.

Constantly ask yourself, "What is the number
one thing I could do in the next 15 minutes
to get me closer to my goal?"
Then do it right away.

Break down large goals into smaller
more manageable goals.

Find a mentor who believes in you,
who will support you, and who will push you
toward your dream.

Don't let others rain on your parade.
Avoid negative people like the plague.

Decide to find the seed of good in every adversity.

Decide that you are willing to do
whatever it takes to realize your dream.

Realize that true happiness lies within you.
Happiness is the product of the quality of your
relationships and of the degree of control you feel
you have in life. Every time you make excuses,
you lose control and become unhappy.

The past does not determine the future.
No matter how many times you have failed,
the next time you could succeed. If you don't
believe it, just read Thomas Edison's biography.

Take full responsibility for your results.

Protect your attitude. Your attitude determines
your altitude. Average talent with great attitude
will beat out great talent with bad attitude
every time.

Read biographies then model your life
after the lives of successful people.

Don't complain about your circumstances.
Decide you will make your own circumstances.

Don't kid yourself. Life is hard.
Success takes time and massive action.

You only live once. Go for the Gold. Decide you
will not simply exist. Decide to live an exciting life.
Don't just take up space. Make a difference
so you will be missed when you are gone.
Decide to leave a legacy.

Be willing to pay the price of success.
No pain no gain.

Vividly imagine what your victory will feel like.
Replay that victory all the time.
It's your preview of coming attractions.

Act in spite of your fear. No guts no glory.

Whenever in doubt, go with the bolder choice.
Base your plan on your strengths.

Humble yourself to the leadership of those
who have done what you want to do.
Ask for help and you will succeed faster.

Believe in yourself. Persist in the face of challenges.
Don't take "No" for an answer.

Celebrate every small victory.

Follow your heart.

Constantly look for ways to simplify your life.

Anger gives people courage to do things they
usually would not do. Whenever you are angry,
don't waste your anger doing negative things.
Harness the energy in your anger to reach your goal.

Embrace change. Change brings opportunity to win.

Know when to listen and know when to speak.
If you're not failing you are playing too safe
and you are not growing. If you want
to succeed faster, double your failure rate.

Bite off more than you can chew.

Live your life with passion.

Read good books, listen to self-development audios,
and attend seminars.

Forgive others quickly. Being angry
at someone else is like drinking poison.

Make your dream so exciting
that it takes your breath away.

Every time you make an excuse you give away
control of your life. Stop making excuses.

Don't live life through others.
Be the hero in your own life.

Watch less TV. Your TV is
keeping you from your dreams.

Establish a mission and a purpose for your life.

Burning desire creates the power to succeed.
Develop a passionate desire for your purpose.
How badly you want it to happen will determine
if you do make it happen.

Never blame, whine or complain.

Talk positively to yourself.
Never bad-mouth or criticize yourself.

Be a good finder. Look for good in everything
that happens. Developing a positive mental attitude
is a decision. A decision that helps you
create a better life.

Fly with eagles, and you'll start to think, feel and
act like an eagle. Hang around with turkeys, and…
well, you get the picture.

Write down your goals every day before
you turn on your computer. It takes less than
two minutes and helps you start off the day
in a more purposeful, focused manner.
Doing this will make you more productive
than 95% of people in the world.

Imitate the perseverance of the people you admire.

Read 15-30 minutes a day from
a positive self-development book.

Become a part of a support group.
Hang out with people who have
goals and dreams similar to yours.

Know yourself. Know your strengths and
weaknesses. That knowledge will help you
understand why you act the way you do.
Learn about the four personality types.

Help others reach their dreams.

See challenges as an opportunity
to become stronger.

Do what you fear and the fear will disappear.

If you want to win big
you have to be willing to lose big.

Focus on your goals, not on your obstacles.

You will only see it when you believe it.

Don't let other people's opinion of you
become your reality.

When the why is big enough,
the how will take care of itself.

If you are not excited about your dream, don't
expect others to get excited about your dream.

Don't listen to the naysayers in your life.
"Impossible" is just the opinion of somebody
who does not believe as much as you do.

Put your dreams in concrete and your plans in sand.

When somebody laughs or makes fun of you,
that person should stop having any influence
in your life. They are holding you back
from your purpose in life.

Whenever somebody compliments you,
they have just seen a glimpse of your greatness.
The compliments you get over and over are a clue
to where your gifts lie. When you use
your God-given gifts to realize your dream,
you make the world a better place.

Associate with big thinkers.
Big people don't laugh at big ideas.

Success is all about guts and vision.
Knowing what you want,
and having the guts to go after it.

As long as you don't quit, you've still got a chance.

You'll either pay the price of success
or the price of regret. The price of success
weighs ounces. The price of regret weighs tons.
It's your choice.

Set high goals for yourself. If you're not
headed anywhere in life, you're headed nowhere.

Wanting to win is not enough.
You have to be willing to prepare to win.

Take more chances. You'll never know
what you were missing in life
until you dare to pursue your dream.

Insanity is doing the same thing and
expecting different results. To get better results
you must constantly adjust your approach.

Fortune favors the brave. Boldness has magic in it.
Don't play it safe. Start taking more chances.

Winners have the courage to get started
and the courage to endure.

Do the things you fear
or else fear will control your life.

Take a leap of faith. Leap and the net will appear.

Commitment creates opportunity.
Stop talking and start doing.
Think less and act more.

The day you take complete responsibility
for yourself, the day you stop making excuses,
is the day you start moving to the top.

Believe that there is an opportunity in every
challenge. Your job is to find it
and to take advantage of it.

If it is to be it is up to you.
Nobody can succeed for you.
You have to make it happen.
There is no one to stop you but yourself.
Decide you will make it happen.

Fear is a smokescreen. Act in spite of your fear
and the fear will disappear.

Invest in yourself. The better you are,
the better your results will be.

Control your thoughts and you control your life.

People of integrity expect to be believed,
and they're willing to let time prove them right.
Be a person of your word.

"If you're going through hell…keep going!"
Winston Churchill

"A good plan, violently executed now
is better than a perfect plan next week."
General George Patton

It's human nature to be lazy – to want to coast.
Therefore, constantly strive to improve, because he
who stops being better eventually stops being good.

You're not finished when you are defeated.
You are only finished when you quit.

The greatest predictor of future success
is how driven and passionate you are to realize your
dream. Passion is much more important than talent.

Have fun. You can't get passionate about anything
if you are not having fun. If you are not having fun
you are probably doing the wrong thing.

Believe that you are the master of your own destiny
and that you can create your own future.

Focus on doing things that will improve your odds
of winning. It's all about improving your odds.

All your actions have consequences.
If you sow massively, you'll reap massively.

There are more opportunities today
than there have ever been.
If you can't make it in the U.S.,
you can't make it anywhere.

If you have an intense desire to achieve something,
it is a given that you have the ability within you.
Your job is to figure out how.

Always expect the best.
We tend to get what we expect.

Be willing to try different approaches on the way
to your goals. If you don't score the touchdown,
don't move the goalposts, change the play.

Create a crystal-clear picture
of what you want to accomplish.

Serve others. Your rewards in life
will be proportionate to the value
of your service to others.

Think about the future instead of the past.
Focus on what you can do today
to improve your future.

Discipline yourself to focus on the solutions,
not on the problems.

Find out what other successful people
in your field are doing, and do the same things
yourself over and over.

Whatever you think about all the time
will grow in your life.

"Work smart, not hard" is a joke. If you truly want
to succeed, you'd better work smart and hard.
The harder you work, the luckier you'll be.

When opportunities appear, move quickly.
Doors of opportunity close as quickly as they open.

You can't do anything about the past,
therefore, remove the words "I should have…"
from your vocabulary. "Should haves,"
create guilt, suck the wind out of your sails,
and drain away positive energy
that you could use to do something
about your problem today.

Constantly ask yourself, "What can I do right now
to reach my goal?" Then, do it right away.

When you move boldly in the direction of your
dreams, unseen forces will come to your aid.

What would you dare to do
if you knew you could not fail?
What are you waiting for? Do it now.

Act as if it were impossible to fail.
Everyone is afraid. Courage is not
the absence of fear. Courage is acting
in spite of your fears. Face your fears
and conquer them with swift action.

Winners understand that the road to success
is filled with failures and challenges.
Winners fail their way to success.
One big success cancels out all the failures.

Assume that success is only a matter of time.
Resolve to learn something from every setback,
and decide that quitting is not an option.

Your persistence will fuel your self-belief
and your self-belief will fuel your persistence.
But you have to decide that quitting
is not an option.

Positive self image does not come
from people praising you.
Confidence and positive self image
comes from competence.
From being good at whatever you do.
And that comes from practice.
Confidence and positive self image
come from constantly facing your fears
and refusing to quit.

Everything you do is either getting you closer or
further from your dream. Everything.

Successful people always talk about
and think about what they want to happen.
Unsuccessful people always talk about and
think about what they don't want to happen.
You attract what you talk about.
What are you talking about?

Make no small plans. Small plans and dreams
don't have the power to inspire and motivate you.
Have a dream that takes your breath away.
Only such a dream will motivate you to act.

Start seeing things and people as they can be,
not as they are.

Winners are willing to do the things
losers are not willing to do.

Think big. Focus on the possibilities,
not on the problems.

The faster you stop operating
from a state of wishful thinking
and get passionately committed to your dream,
the better your life will be.

Limiting what you are willing to do
limits what you will achieve.

The books you read and the people
you associate with will determine
where you are in five years.

You determine your habits.
Your habits determine your future.

Nothing of value comes without effort.
Decide you'll do whatever it takes.
Decide you are willing to pay the price.

The secret of your future
is hidden in your daily routine.

High achievers have a drive that most of us can't
even begin to imagine. They work every day at
catching their breaks. They are ordinary people
with extraordinary drive and work ethic.
You can develop the same drive.

Success is a decision. It's all up to you.

Once a year, read "How to Win Friends and
Influence People," "The Magic of Thinking
Big," and "The Power of Positive Thinking."

Every morning, get in front of the bathroom mirror,
and serious as a heart attack,
tell yourself what your dreams and goals are.
Repeat this every time you are in front of a mirror.
Do this and in time you will become unstoppable.

Develop people and leadership skills.
The only way to accomplish great goals
is by building a team and
working through other people.

What you believe will determine what you will do.
What you do determines your results.
Change your beliefs,
and you'll change your results.

When you work hard enough and long enough
that you start believing that you deserve to succeed,
you'll start acting like a deserving person and
success will come to you.

When you achieve your dream, pursue another
dream. That's how to live a life of adventure.

Understand this about the steepness of the slope as
you approach the summit of any competition.
Be it luge in the Olympics, basketball in the NBA,
or being the most successful business in your field.
There's as much difference between number 10
in the world and number 5 as there is between
number 100 and number 10. Going from number 5
to 4 is the same like going from 10 to 5.
And from 3 on up it is inconceivable.
What that means is that whenever you plateau
at any level and you want to get to the next level,
you'd better be willing to put forth
much more effort.

Don't let other people's weakness
get in the way of your strengths
and rob you of your dream.

A dream gives you energy, hope,
and keeps you from wasting your life.

If you have no critics,
you likely have no successes.

Success is a decision. You decide to do
whatever it takes for as long as it takes to make it.

Your ability to succeed is in direct proportion
to your ability to take rejection.

Levels of commitment – I'll try, I'll do my best,
I'll do whatever it takes, it's a done deal.

Big people don't laugh at big ideas.

The only thing in life
which does not require effort is failure.

Learn to love the struggle.

Double your failure rate. Failure is the best teacher.
Success lies just on the other side of failure.

Find a dream big enough to overcome your fears.

Plant with bold faith
and stay around for the harvest.

Show up for practice.
Champions show up for practice.

People who make excuses have no direction in life.
No dream. They don't know where they are going.

Go from one failure to another
without losing enthusiasm.
Go from one success to another
without losing humility.

Mental toughness – Have fun, focus on the task
at hand, be passionate, bounce back from failures.

Every time you do something you fear,
every time you step up and look fear in the face,
you gain strength, confidence, courage, and faith.

The struggle, the sacrifice (giving up something
good today for something better tomorrow)
of doing the right thing ennobles you.
Behaviors do not just serve our physical needs,
they serve our spiritual needs as well.

You don't have to justify your actions.

The reward for doing right is mostly internal;
self-respect, dignity, integrity, and self-esteem.
Doing right gives you a sense of order,
calm, and peace. You sleep better.

Seize the day, accept responsibility for the future,
chase your dream, never quit,
and people will say you are lucky.

The 95% rule says – There's a 95% chance
that 95% of everything you know
about life and business and success
has come from people in the bottom 95% group.
If that is true (and it is), then how do you expect
to get top 5% results? That's why you need
to hang around the top 5% group.

The will that weakens first strengthens the other.
If you back down from something you fear,
the fear for that thing gets stronger.
If you boldly face you fear, you get stronger.

Don't assume anything.
Get the specific information.
Assuming sets you up to be a fool later.

Keep your eye on the target
and look for different ways to reach it.

If you talk about it, it's a dream…
if you plan it, it's possible…
when you take action, it's real
and it starts to change your life.

Set people up to win. Especially in the beginning.
In the beginning, people's actions are very limited
because they think they have limited potential
(they can't see themselves far into the future).
If you have limited belief,
you are going to use limited potential,
and you are going to take limited action.
That's why you break goals down
into manageable tasks.
To keep the belief your level high.

You can't win if you're not in the game.

There is dignity in being willing to fight.
Dignity in being willing to take the journey.

You have a noble purpose in life. Figure out
what it is and dedicate your life to it.

Your support team is a constant source
of power and strength.

Protect and nourish your dream.
Protect your attitude. That is the basis of success.

A movie without a challenge to overcome
and a destination to reach is boring.
The same is true about a life with
no goals or challenges to overcome.
In order for life to be an adventure
there must be a goal.

Being great means being misunderstood.
Don't ever fear being misunderstood.

The more you persist in the face of adversity,
the more you like and respect yourself.

Take full responsibility of the job you do.
It is a reflection of you.

Face your fears and do it anyways.

Don't worry about what others think about you.
What matters is knowing who you are
and believing the possibilities for your life.

Focus on the possibilities
and take control of your own destiny.

Don't waste your anger. Whenever you get mad
at something, learn to channel that anger
in a positive way. Passion is positive anger.
All progress comes from people who are mad and
dissatisfied. They are sick and tired
of being sick and tired.

We're not living in the agricultural age
or in the industrial age. We're living in the
information age. The people armed with the best
information and willing to apply it will win.
That's why the people you associate with
and the books you read will determine your destiny.
Are you reading the books that will help you
realize your dreams? Are you associating
with the people who will help you
realize your dreams? If you're not,
you're fooling yourself.

The size of a person's bank account is proportional
to the size of a person's library.
Poor people have big TVs and no books.
Rich people have small TVs and huge libraries.
They're too busy applying what they learn
to have time to watch TV.
TV is the electronic income reducer.

Most people feel trapped in their circumstances.
They don't realize they have the power to change.
Fear holds them back.

There is a part of us that wants to have
passion, hope, optimism and energy.
The part that is sick of having to put up
with the roles assigned by the world.
The part that does not want to be controlled.
The part of us that is genuine,
yet the part of us that usually lives in silence.

Most people are not living the life they want
or the life that they would choose.
Most people live a life that pleases other people
but not themselves. Their hearts are not in it.
It is not natural. So everything is a chore.
There is no passion, no excitement.

People ignore their real dreams.
Being someone you are not
is the hardest thing you will ever do.

Most people don't allow themselves
to be themselves. And by doing that,
they cheat themselves and they cheat everyone else.
And yet since it feels safe, they persist in living life
with that dull ache inside.

If it does not come from your heart
it is not really you. And it won't be fun.
So take that leap of faith and go for it.
If you jump the net will appear.

If you will embrace and consistently and
persistently apply these principles,
you will amaze people with all you accomplish.
People will say you are lucky
but you'll know luck had nothing to do with it.

Chase your dream. Never Quit.

About Ruben Gonzalez

A seemingly "ordinary guy," Ruben wasn't a gifted athlete. He didn't take up the sport of luge until he was 21. Against all odds, four years and a few broken bones later, he was competing in the Calgary Winter Olympics. At the age of 47 he was racing against 20-year-olds at the Vancouver Olympics. His story takes people's excuses away.

Ruben's an outstanding storyteller with an incredible story that inspires audiences to think differently, live life with passion, and to push beyond self-imposed limitations and to produce Olympic-caliber results.

Ruben's appeared nationally on ABC, CBS, NBC, CNN, and FOX. He's been featured in Time Magazine, Success Magazine, The New York Times, as well as publications all over the world. Ruben's the author of the critically acclaimed book, "The Courage to Succeed."

Ruben speaks from both Olympic and business experience. Before becoming a professional speaker, Ruben was a top producing copier salesman in Houston, Texas.

As a speaker, Ruben has shared the stage with Zig Ziglar, Tom Hopkins and Denis Waitley. Ruben's client list reads like a Who's Who of Corporate America. He's spoken for audiences around the world; Europe, Africa, Asia, North and South America.

Ruben's presentation is an Olympic experience his audiences never forget. See for yourself, watch his demo video on his website. You'll like it so much, you'll want your whole family to watch it.

Ruben lives in Colorado with his wife Cheryl and their children Gabriela and Gracen. He enjoys the challenge of climbing Colorado's fourteen-thousand-foot peaks, snowboarding, sailing and flying.

What Top Achievers are Saying About Ruben's Presentations

"Invite Ruben to speak
to your group
You'll be glad you did."

- Zig Ziglar

"Ruben is a great speaker; funny, quick-witted, and he has an incredible story to boot."

- Dave Ramsey

"Ruben's incredible story inspires people to be their best."

- Howard Putnam,
Former CEO Southwest Airlines

Join the Thousands of high achievers who have learned how to become unstoppable on the way to success.

Sign up for Ruben's Success Tips.

To subscribe, Visit

RubenTips.com

Watch dozens of Ruben's personal development videos here

RubenTV.com

"Success is like wrestling a gorilla You don't quit when you're tired. You quit when the gorilla is tired!"

- Robert Strauss